Elijah went before the people and said,
"How long will you waver between
two opinions? If the Lord is God,
follow Him; but if Baal is god,
follow him."
1 Kings 18:21 NIV

To Erik

ELIJAH
Prophet of Fire
Retold by Anne de Graaf
Illustrated by José Pérez Montero
© Copyright 1991 by Scandinavia Publishing House
Nørregade 32, DK-1165 Copenhagen K

English-language edition published through
special arrangement with Scandinavia by
Wm. B. Eerdmans Publishing Co.,
255 Jefferson Ave. S.E., Grand Rapids, Michigan 49503
Printed in Hong Kong

ISBN 0-8028-5038-3

ELIJAH
Prophet of Fire

Written by Anne de Graaf
Illustrated by José Pérez Montero

Eerdmans

A very long time ago there lived a wicked queen. Her name was Jezebel. She was married to the Israelite king Ahab. Jezebel was very evil and very powerful. There was only one man who dared to fight Jezebel. This brave man was called Elijah.

Elijah had been chosen by God to speak His words to His people, the Israelites. This meant Elijah was a prophet for God.

Jezebel did not even believe in God. She came from a people who worshiped statues of false gods. The Lord God had ordered His people to pray to no one but Him. When King Ahab married Jezebel, he started worshiping her false gods instead. This was very, very wrong. It broke God's first Commandment to His people, that they should only worship the one true God.

Evil Queen Jezebel even tried to kill the Lord's prophets. Then she told Ahab to make his people stop praying to God. "Tell them I have killed all their prophets! Tell them they must worship my gods!"

Ahab did whatever his wife wanted. He built places to worship Jezebel's false gods. He made the people pray and burn sacrifices there. And the people did what their king wanted.

Because of this terrible thing, Jezebel and Ahab became known as the most evil king and queen God's people ever had.

Everyone was very afraid of Jezebel, everyone except Elijah. Jezebel always tried to kill her enemies. When she tried to kill the prophets of the Lord, though, at least one man escaped. That one man was Elijah.

Elijah knew Jezebel would be hunting him. Yet he felt God pushing him to speak with Ahab. Elijah was God's prophet. It was his job to tell people what God wanted them to hear.

Elijah went to the royal palace. There he warned Ahab, "You must stop worshiping these false gods. You've made the people stop praying to God. He will punish you for this!"

Ahab swallowed. "I was just doing what my wife told me. There's nothing wrong with the people praying to statues. Who could it harm? God won't notice."

But God had noticed. Elijah told him, "The Lord God is going to make your land dry up like a desert! He will not let the rain fall again until I ask Him to!" Then Elijah left the palace.

God told Elijah to hide in the hills. Elijah was alone, but God took care of him. Elijah drank water from a nearby stream. When he was hungry, big black birds called ravens brought him food. Every day the ravens brought Elijah meat and bread.

While the rest of the country was going hungry and thirsty, Elijah had plenty to eat and drink. This lasted a long time, until one day, the stream finally dried up.

When there was no more water in the stream, Elijah asked God what he should do. The Lord told him, "Go to a village near the place where Jezebel comes from. You will find a woman whose husband is dead. She will give you food."

Elijah did as God told him. He looked very strange as he entered the village. Many people stared at Elijah. He had been living for months in the desert and looked like a wild man! His hair was long and he wore animal skins as his clothes.

When he spoke to the widow, though, she did not run away. "Would you please give me a little water and some bread?" he asked her.

The woman shook her head sadly. "I have nothing." She looked down at the firewood in her arms. "I was going to use this wood to make a fire for my last meal. My son and I have nothing left but a little flour and oil. I was going to make a little bread from that.

That will be our last meal, and then we will starve to death." The woman did not look up.

Elijah asked God what he could do. God told him. Elijah said softly, "Don't be afraid. Make the bread. Then give some to me. The Lord God will make sure your flour and oil do not run out until He sends rain to this place again."

It had been a very long time since there was any rain. Even King Ahab and Queen Jezebel did not have enough to drink. But they still refused to believe God could help them.

When this woman heard Elijah's promise, she could hardly believe her ears. "How is it possible?" she asked herself. Unlike Ahab and Jezebel, though, she chose to believe God could help her. "Yes," she nodded to Elijah. "Yes, come home with me and I will feed you."

She did not know how it had happened, but the widow believed the promise this strange man of God had made to her.

That evening, when the flour and oil were almost all gone, her son shouted, "Mother! Mother! Look, the jar is full of oil again! And the bowl of flour is full, too! Didn't you say it was all gone?"

The woman smiled. "This is a miracle. That man of God said it would happen like this."

Elijah came down the stairs and heard her. "Listen to your mother," he said to the boy. "It is a miracle, God's way of taking care of people when they listen and believe."

From that day on, there was always oil in the jar and flour in the bowl. Day after day the woman had enough food for her son and for Elijah. The prophet came to live with the widow and she fed him and gave him a place to sleep.

Elijah had no family of his own. As he stayed with the widow and her son, he grew fond of the boy. He prayed for him and taught him about the Lord.

Then one day, the widow's son became very sick. He had been starving to death before Elijah came to live with him and his mother. So he was already very weak when he became ill.

Now the boy grew weaker and weaker. Finally he died in his mother's arms. The woman had already lost her husband. Now her son was dead.

She cried out to Elijah, "Why? Why me? You said your God would take care of us. Why am I being punished? Look at my son! He's dead!"

"Here, give him to me," Elijah said. He gently took the boy into his own arms. Elijah carried the boy upstairs to his room, while the mother stayed downstairs, sobbing.

Elijah laid the boy on his own bed. Then he leaned over him and prayed. "Dear God, have You brought so much sadness into this home, where I am staying?"

Elijah did a very strange thing. He stretched himself out on the boy three times. He prayed, "My Lord God, let this boy's life come back to him!" Three times Elijah begged God to make the boy live again. He asked God with all his heart.

And then, suddenly, Elijah felt the boy's body growing warmer under him. He gasped and looked at the child's face. His eyes fluttered open. The boy looked at Elijah. Then he smiled!

"You're alive," Elijah whispered to his little friend. He held him close and said a prayer of thanks to God. The Lord had heard Elijah's cries. The boy was alive!

Elijah picked up the boy again and brought him to his mother. "Look, your son is alive!"

The mother wiped the tears from her eyes. She shivered. "No, but," she started to say. Then she saw her son smiling at her.

Again she started crying. This time these were happy tears. As she put her arms around Elijah and her boy, the woman said, "Now I know you are a man of God. The messages you speak from God are the truth. Just look, my son is alive!"

Elijah stayed with the widow and her son for three years. All that time the rest of the country grew drier and drier. It had been a very long time since any rain had fallen. The land became a desert. Many people had no food. No one had any water. All the rivers and streams and lakes had dried up. The only water was in the sea, and they could not drink that.

As the years without rain dragged on, Jezebel grew more and more furious. "This is all your fault!" the evil queen yelled at her husband.

Ahab sent soldiers to comb the country for Elijah. Meanwhile Queen Jezebel had again ordered her soldiers to kill all the Lord's prophets. "That will teach their God to dry up our land!" Only a hundred managed to escape.

When Elijah was finally found, Ahab went to see him. He said, "You troublemaker, Elijah! Thanks to you, there's been no rain for three years!"

"I am not the troublemaker," Elijah said. "You are. You chose to worship Jezebel's gods. The Lord sent no rain so you would learn He is the one and only God. Now I will show you how worthless your false gods are! Bring eight hundred of Jezebel's priests to the top of Mount Carmel. There we will have a contest!"

A few days later Ahab and Jezebel's priests arrived for the contest. A huge crowd of Israelites were watching. Elijah told them, "Now you will have to choose between the Lord God and Baal! Watch and see if Baal can set on fire the wood and bull you have offered in front of his statue. Just see if he listens!"

The priests of Baal danced and prayed and sang and yelled and even cut themselves. But no fire fell from heaven.

13

Elijah laughed at Baal's priests, "Maybe you should shout louder! This god of yours might be thinking, or busy or traveling or sleeping! Ha, ha!"

Still nothing happened. Then it was Elijah's turn. Elijah turned to the people. "Do you know why nothing happened? Because Baal is a nothing god! God wants to prove to you that He alone is God, there is no one else!"

Elijah set up his own offering to the Lord. He repaired the Lord's altar which Jezebel's priests had destroyed. He dug a hole around the altar and laid stones around the trench. He placed the wood and dead bull on top of the altar.

Then Elijah poured four jars of water onto the altar! He did this three times. The people gasped, "How can it possibly catch fire now that it is wet?"

Elijah heard them. "Now you will know God is the only God. No one but the Lord could light this with fire now that I have soaked it in water."

Elijah started praying. "Lord God, show these people that You are the true God of Israel. Send fire from heaven, I pray!"

Then, with a mighty "swoosh!" fire rained down from the sky! The water-soaked wood and meat were burned in a mighty fire. The crowd shouted, "The Lord is God! The Lord is God!"

Elijah cried out, "Now do you believe that only the Lord is the true God?"

The people had fallen to their knees. "Yes, yes, we believe!" Elijah told the people to capture Jezebel's priests so he could kill them all.

Once he had done that, Elijah prayed for rain. Again he wanted to show the Israelites how powerful God was. Again, God answered Elijah's prayers. Soon rain fell on the thirsty land.

The people raised their hands and cheered. At last, once they believed in God, He had sent them rain!

Elijah hoped with all his heart that the people would remember what they had seen that day.

Later, wicked Jezebel heard what had happened on Mount Carmel. "He did what?" she screamed at Ahab. "He killed my priests? Well, you tell Elijah that now I'm going to kill him!"

When Elijah heard about Jezebel's threat, he ran for his life. Before he left the city, though, he saw a group of women worshiping one of Jezebel's false gods. "Oh Lord, they've forgotten You already!" Elijah cried.

He hid in the desert and felt very tired and upset. An angel of the Lord came to give him food and water. "Rest, and you will feel better," the angel said.

Then Elijah traveled deeper into the desert until he reached a cave. There he fell to the ground, very afraid and very sad.

Elijah fell asleep inside the cave. He felt lost and alone. Suddenly, he heard the Voice of God say, "Elijah, why are you here?"

Elijah woke up with a start. "Oh Lord, I knew You would hear my prayers. I've tried my hardest to show Your people they should only pray to You. But no matter how many miracles happen, they still won't listen. Jezebel has killed Your prophets. I'm all alone. And now she wants to kill me, too!" Elijah had lost all hope.

The Lord said, "I want you to wait for Me. I will pass by you and make you feel stronger." This was an amazing thing! The Lord Himself was going to appear to Elijah!

So Elijah waited. First came a mighty wind. It blasted through the mountains and split the rocks apart. But the Lord was not in the wind. Then came a frightening earthquake. But the Lord was not in the earthquake.

Then came a fire which burnt everything for miles around. But the Lord was not in the fire.

And then, as soft as a breeze, there came the sound of a gentle whisper. Elijah looked up. He covered his face with his cloak and walked out to the entrance of the cave.

Elijah complained again to the Lord. "The people won't listen! I'm all alone! And now Jezebel wants to kill me, too!" He thought his life was almost over.

The Lord had plans for Elijah, though. "No, Elijah, your life is not almost over. Rest for a while in the desert. Then go to Damascus. There I will show you your helper, a young man named Elisha. Then you won't be so alone."

This made Elijah feel much better. He smiled. The Lord had known just what Elijah most needed, a helper.

So Elijah stayed in the desert for a while. Then he traveled to Damascus and did as God had told him. He went looking for Elisha.

Even though the two men had names which sounded alike, they were different. Elijah was much older than Elisha. Elijah was a wild-looking prophet who wandered the land telling people about God.

Elisha was a farmer. When Elijah found Elisha, he was plowing a field with a pair of oxen. Elijah called to him. He put his cloak around Elisha's shoulders. It was a way of showing Elisha he had been chosen to follow and learn from Elijah.

Elisha knew what it meant. "Please, may I say good-bye to my parents? Then I will follow you." Elijah agreed as Elisha told his friends and family about the exciting thing which had happened to him.

In the years to come Elisha was a great help to Elijah. He took care of Elijah. And he watched and learned from him, so that someday, Elisha would be able to become a prophet for the Lord, just like Elijah.

All this time the wicked queen Jezebel was still causing trouble. She continued to make her husband Ahab force the Israelites to worship her false gods. And Jezebel swore that if she ever did find Elijah, she would kill him!

Elijah knew this, but he was not afraid. Now he had young Elisha at his side. The Lord had made Elijah stronger. Together, the two men wandered the country telling people not to listen to Jezebel.

"Her gods are nothing. Pray to the Lord God instead. He loves you and wants to help you, but you must believe in Him and not

these statues!" Some people listened, but very few believed.

By now, Ahab was a very selfish king. Whenever he saw something he wanted, he took it. This happened once when King Ahab saw a vineyard he wanted. It was right next to the palace. He called the owner, a man named Naboth.

"Sell me your vineyard. I want it!"

"I cannot sell you that land. It belonged to my father and my grandfather and before that, to his father," Naboth said.

But Ahab would not listen. He went home and complained to the queen. She laughed at him and told him, "Don't worry! I'll make sure you get your vineyard."

Ahab's evil wife did just that. She paid two men to tell lies about Naboth. She had him arrested. These two men made up horrible stories about Naboth. Finally the men of the city dragged Naboth out to the city walls and stoned him to death.

Once poor Naboth was dead, Jezebel sent for Ahab. "I've had that man killed, the one who would not sell you his land. Now you can have his vineyard." Jezebel laughed.

Thanks to Jezebel's lies, Ahab had what he wanted. But God had seen how a good man had been killed. He sent Elijah to talk to the king.

"The Lord has seen how Jezebel murdered a man so you could steal his land," Elijah told Ahab. Ahab turned pale. "The Lord says that when you and your family die, the dogs will lick up your blood."

Ahab knew he had done something very evil. But Elijah was not finished. He knew that if Jezebel found him near the palace she would surely have him killed. But he was not afraid. The Lord had given Elijah a message for Ahab. Elijah had spent his whole life speaking God's words to people. He wasn't about to stop now.

"And when Jezebel dies, she will be eaten by dogs, here right near her own palace. That is the Lord's punishment for you and your wife." Ahab realized what a terrible thing he had done and felt very sorry, but it was too late.

Much later, while Ahab was fighting in a battle, he was hit by an arrow. He died while riding in his chariot. After Ahab was buried, a soldier was cleaning the king's chariot when he noticed some dogs licking up Ahab's blood. Everything Elijah had said would happen, came true.

During this time Israel was fighting many battles against many tribes. King Ahab died during a battle against Aram. But Israel was also fighting against another country where God's own people were living, called Judah. This was tragic. Two of the twelve tribes of God's people who should have been worshiping the same God were killing each other.

Again, though, it was because Jezebel and Ahab were such wicked leaders. Over and over again they had made the Israelites fight battles against other tribes, including their own people! Most of the time it was because they wanted more treasure or land, because they were so selfish.

When Ahab died in battle, his son Ahaziah became king. Ahaziah was even more evil than his father. He did everything his wicked mother told him to. And Ahaziah was never sorry.

But the worst thing about Ahaziah was that he always worshiped the false god Baal. Just like his mother, he told the people they should not listen to Elijah. But Ahaziah was very, very wrong.

One day, the king had a bad accident. Ahaziah fell from the roof and was badly hurt. He ordered his servants to find the priests of Baal. "Find out if I'm going to die," he told them.

But on the way, these servants met Elijah. "Tell the king the Lord wants to know why he looks for answers from a false god like Baal. The Lord God knows what will happen to King Ahaziah. Tell him God says he will die from his injuries!"

When the servants heard this, they hurried back to the palace. They told the king what had happened. "What?" the king roared. "My mother told me about this Elijah. He caused a great deal of trouble for her and my father. Now he has bad news for me. I know one way of making sure he never bothers us again.

"You there," he pointed at an officer of the guard. "Take fifty men and capture Elijah."

The officer found Elijah praying on top of a hill. "Man of God, come with us!" he ordered.

Elijah called out, "If I am a man of God, then may fire fall from heaven and kill you!" Suddenly, fire rained down on the soldiers, killing them all.

The king sent another fifty men to take Elijah, but the same thing happened. When the third fifty men came to Elijah's hill, the captain fell to his knees. "Please," he begged Elijah. "Please, have mercy on us."

An angel from God told Elijah, "Go with him and do not be afraid."

So Elijah listened and did as the angel told him. Once in the palace, Elijah told Ahaziah, "You should have trusted God. Why didn't you ask Him if you were going to get better? Why do you trust Baal more than the Lord? Why? Because you are very bad. You are even worse than your father. Yes, you are going to die!"

And it happened just as Elijah had said it would.

All his life Elijah fought the evil Jezebel, trying to lead the Israelites back to God. When Jezebel finally died, she was pushed from a balcony and fell to the ground. By the time people found her next to the palace, dogs had already eaten her up. It was a terrible ending for a terrible queen.

Elijah taught Elisha everything he knew. They were like father and son. When Elijah was very, very old, he and Elisha walked into the desert together.

Elijah told Elisha, "You stay here. I must go away."

"But I will never leave you," young Elisha said. He was sad because he knew that the Lord was going to take Elijah away.

Some prophets followed the men, but Elisha and Elijah left them behind when they reached the River Jordan. There, Elijah took off his cloak and hit the water. The river split in two and the men crossed the river on dry ground.

Once on the other side a golden chariot of fire suddenly blazed through the sky! Fiery horses pulled it down from heaven. Elijah climbed into the chariot and was taken away from Elisha.

"My father! My father! Oh, now you are gone!" Elisha cried out as the fiery whirlwind carried Elijah, the prophet of fire up to heaven to be with God.

Elijah stayed in heaven for many, many

years. Then, during the time that Jesus walked the earth, Elijah came back from heaven to talk with Jesus. The message Elijah preached all his life was true then, and is still true today. No one or nothing should be more important to God's people than praying to the one true Lord God.

31

You can find the story of Elijah in the Old Testament book of First Kings, chapters 16 to the end and the first two chapters of Second Kings.